American Heroes

Stephen Mansfield

American Heroes

Copyright © 2006 by Stephen Mansfield

Published by the J. Countryman® division of the Thomas Nelson Book Group,
Nashville, Tennessee

J. Countryman® is a trademark of Thomas Nelson, Inc.
Scripture quotations are taken from *The Holy Bible*, New King James Version © 1979, 1980, 1982, 1992, by Thomas Nelson, Inc. Used by permission.

Project Editor: Lisa Stilwell

Designed by Jay Smith, Juicebox Designs, Nashville, TN www.juiceboxdesigns.com
Cover photograph by Mark DeLong, DeLong Photography, Nashville, TN www.delongphoto.com

ISBN 1-4041-0416-X

Printed and bound in the United States

www.jcountryman.com I www.thomasnelson.com

Table of Contents

**PAR AVION
VIA AIR MAIL**

Introduction

They weren't supposed to be heroes. In fact, many experts doubted they would even be normal. They were supposed to be part of that troubled generation, the one that came of age around the dawn of the millennium. Some nicknamed them the Millennials and others called them Generation Y, but no one expected they would amount to much.

They were the Columbine generation, after all. Mall rats and latch key kids. Older generations thought of them as the spoiled offspring of guilt-ridden baby-boomer parents who plied them with toys but never told them who they really were. And when they went off to the battlefields of Afghanistan and Iraq, many at home doubted that this new generation would be able to understand the war on terror, much less fight it effectively. As one sergeant said, "All the media seemed to hope for us was that we would somehow kill more of the enemy than we would our own soldiers."

Then these Millennials, these twenty-somethings, began to fight. And they did it magnificently. Commanders reported that these new warriors were the most patriotic, best educated, and most effective fighting force they had ever seen. Even the media saw it. As one journalist in Iraq reported, "The press back home doesn't have it right.

We are doing these people a disservice. I came over here expecting *Animal House* and *Debbie Does Dallas*. What I found was *Braveheart* and *Saving Private Ryan*."

Something had happened. Perhaps it was the horror of September 11, 2001, or a generation rising to its country's need, or maybe simply a chance to fight for something more than a parking space at the mall. Whatever it was, it was obvious that these millennial warriors had changed in a way that defied both their history and their critics.

Before long the stories began making their way home. The hero tales. They were lost at first behind the more controversial sagas of Abu Ghraib and Guantanamo Bay. Yet when the dust of scandal settled, the monuments of greatness were revealed. And they were heartrending. The nation heard of soldiers who gave themselves for their friends, common men who did the uncommon in the heat of battle. America learned that heroism was not dead among its young.

Hero. It is a word that had fallen out of fashion for a time. Then Ronald Reagan began to use it, often as he pointed to some courageous fireman or public school teacher sitting in the gallery while he addressed Congress. This reenergized the word in our language. It took 9/11 to restore both the word and the ideal to our national life. America understood what heroism was when firemen raced up burning buildings or secretaries gave their lives to show others the way of escape. Almost instantly, the ideal of the hero was restored to its rightful place of honor.

Not long after, the new generation at war began living out that ideal on the battlefields of Afghanistan and Iraq. And the hero tales came, the near legendary deeds of courage and sacrifice.

Now Americans have begun to understand what these tales can mean. They are not just war stories, simple sagas of violence and blood. Rather, they are torches of inspiration that shine on the altar of national honor. They are lessons in character, a summons to be the best that America can be.

Read them, these tales of heroism. Take them strongly to heart. Let them ignite a fire of inspiration that will leave the nation forever changed and the American soldiers who lived them forever honored by the heroes of a new generation.

IT DOESN'T TAKE

ORDER MEN INTO BATTLE

TO **BE ONE** OF

WHO GOES INTO BATTLE.

NORMAN SCHWARZKOPF

Captain
WITH A
Cause

Russell Rippetoe had been disappointed that memorable day when his unit's plane landed on the runway at Baghdad International Airport. He was a Ranger, after all, a member of the famed Seventy-fifth Ranger Regiment made famous in the film *Black Hawk Down*. He had wanted to arrive in Iraq by parachute. "I wanted to jump to see if I could hold up to the stress," he wrote in his journal, "and do my job to the standard of all the Rangers."

But then Russell Rippetoe was always striving to be his best. At home he had been a soccer star, the homecoming king at his Colorado high school, and an Eagle Scout. His plan had been to fly planes for the air force but a minor form of dyslexia killed that dream.

Instead, he got his degree from the University of Colorado and joined the army. Rippetoe had found a home. After getting some help from army doctors for his dyslexia, he became a Ranger and joined the famed Eighty-second Airborne at Fort Bragg. He told his father, a retired Vietnam veteran, that he had found his destiny.

After landing in Iraq, Captain Rippetoe gave himself to his nation's cause. And that is what he was doing on April 3, 2003, when he and five of his men were guarding a checkpoint near a strategic dam outside of Baghdad. On that day three white Suburbans appeared. Captain Rippetoe, sensing something odd, told his men to hold back. As he approached the Suburbans, a woman stepped from one of them and began screaming, "I'm hungry! I need food and water!" Rippetoe moved forward to see how he could help. That was the signal. The driver in one of the other Suburbans detonated a bomb that blew a house-sized hole in the earth. Captain Russell Rippetoe and two of his men were killed. The others were wounded but they survived to tell the tale of their captain's courage.

Then began the grieving—and the haunting sense of destiny. When Rippetoe's father traveled to Fort Benning, Georgia, to clean out his dead son's locker, he found a note the young officer had written before shipping out. "I want a military funeral," he had written, "and I want it to be with my people."

So the Rangers buried one of their own and Captain Russell Rippetoe became the first man killed in Iraq to be buried at Arlington National Cemetery. Just a few weeks after the funeral, President Bush honored Rippetoe in his Memorial Day speech. "This faithful army captain," the president intoned, "has joined a noble company of service and sacrifice gathered row on row. These men and women were strong and courageous and not dismayed. And we pray that they have found their peace in the arms of God."

The SOLDIER,

above all other men, is required to practice
THE GREATEST ACT OF RELIGIOUS
TRAINING—SACRIFICE.

In battle and in the face of danger and death,
HE DISCLOSES THOSE DIVINE
ATTRIBUTES WHICH HIS
MAKER GAVE when He created man in
His own image. No physical courage and no
brute instinct can take the place of the divine
help which alone can sustain him.

General Douglas MacArthur

GRACE on the BATTLEFIELD

It was Christmas morning in Baghdad and "Sergeant C"* was leading an assault squad to clean up a nest of insurgents. Small arms fire broke out, and Sergeant C decided to round a corner and take stock of the situation he and his men were in.

As he did, he found himself quite literally looking into the barrel of a 9mm automatic pistol. Before the sergeant could react, the Iraqi soldier holding the pistol pulled the trigger. Though he remembered thinking he was about to die, the sergeant soon found himself still standing. Assuming the gun had misfired, he immediately advanced on the Iraqi soldier who, now in shock himself, instantly surrendered.

When the mission was complete, Sergeant C felt lightheaded. Fellow soldiers saw blood around his mouth and urged him to quickly get to the clinic. On the way, the sergeant realized one of his teeth was missing. He assumed the ballistic shock from the pistol had knocked the tooth loose. He was wrong. When he arrived at the clinic, X-rays revealed that the Iraqi's gun had not misfired but had instead implanted a bullet exactly where the missing tooth had been. The bullet had apparently entered just below Sergeant C's nose and then positioned itself in place of the missing tooth. Army dentists easily removed the bullet and Sergeant C returned to his unit, taunted by his comrades for the temporary lisp the missing tooth gave him.

When this amazing story was circulated in e-mails and retold in the *Army Times*, it became a source of inspiration to thousands in the field. The story was pinned on bulletin boards and folded into helmets, this tale of what many took to be God's grace on the battlefield.

*The full name of Sergeant C cannot be given for security reasons.

Even in war, moral power
is to physical
as three parts out of four.

"GOD, ARE YOU ABLE TO

PROTECT ME OVER HERE?"

THE MESSAGE
of a MISSILE

On a cool, quiet January morning, Corporal Rick Garrett was shaving in the shower trailer at Camp Victory, Iraq. Wrapped in a towel and enjoying the energy he felt from a good night's sleep, he began thinking about the months he had left overseas. Many questions filled his mind: Would the war get even bloodier? Would any of his buddies be killed? Would he do his duty well? In fact, would he even survive?

Then another question—it was a prayer, really—formed itself in his mind: "God, are you able to protect me over here?"

The words had just become a conscious thought when Corporal Garrett heard a deafening crash. It was the sound of the trailer door shattering. An RPG (rocket-propelled grenade) had pierced the door and was now flying through the middle of the trailer. In an instant, the projectile flew past

Corporal Garrett, lightly creasing his stomach en route, and embedded itself in the trailer wall opposite the door.

For a moment, Garrett was frozen in shock, expecting the RPG to explode. But it did not. Realizing he might have a moment to escape, the corporal ran to the gaping hole where the door had been and hurled himself through it to the ground several feet below. Jumping up as quickly as he could, he sprinted from the trailer while shouting a warning to those in the nearby trailers. Dozens of soldiers braced themselves for an explosion.

Yet nothing happened. The RPG never exploded. It was a dud. Garrett picked himself up from the ground and began laughing with relief. As a crowd gathered and began congratulating him for his luck, he remembered the question he had been asking God: "Can you protect me over here?" It seemed that God had answered.

In case the message hadn't been clear enough, though, there was something more. When the ordinance specialists examined the unexploded RPG, they found a message had been scratched onto it. This was not uncommon. Insurgents often painted or scratched some message on the missiles they fired as an added insult to their American enemy. But the message on this particular missile had a special meaning to Corporal Garrett.

It read simply, "From the God of the American Soldiers."

Apparently, an insurgent had intended the message as a cruel insult. Corporal Garrett knew better. Whatever the insurgents meant to say, he knew that his God was saying, in dramatic terms, "Yes, I can protect you over here. For I am indeed, 'the God of the American Soldiers.'"

You shall not be afraid of the terror by night,
Nor of the arrow that flies by day,
Nor of the pestilence that walks in darkness,
Nor of the destruction that lays waste at noonday.

Psalm 91:5-6

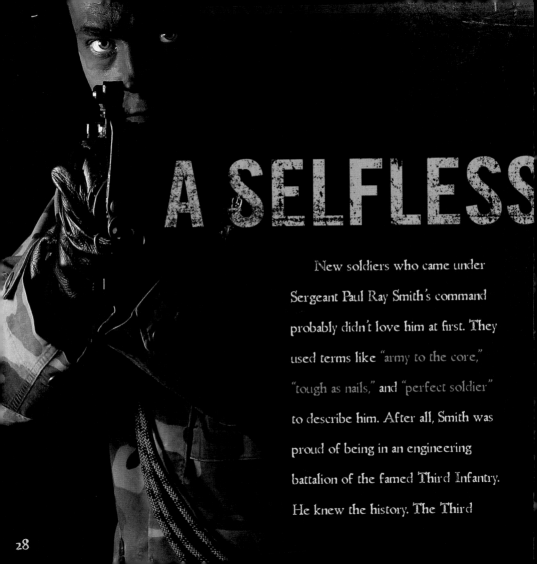

A SELFLESS

New soldiers who came under Sergeant Paul Ray Smith's command probably didn't love him at first. They used terms like "army to the core," "tough as nails," and "perfect soldier" to describe him. After all, Smith was proud of being in an engineering battalion of the famed Third Infantry. He knew the history. The Third

AMERICAN

Infantry had earned the name "Rock of the Marne" in a famous battle outside of Paris during World War I and had enhanced their fighting reputation during World War II. Sergeant Paul Ray Smith had no intention of letting his men live beneath that heroic heritage. So he was tough: "Army all the way," they said.

Eventually, they would come to see another side of this man. One time, for instance, just a few days after the invasion of Iraq, Sergeant Smith crawled on his hands and knees into an Iraqi minefield to guarantee his men's safety. He could have assigned that duty to someone else. Instead, he did it himself and his men came to love him for it.

On April 4, 2003, Sergeant Smith's men came to love him even more. Their unit's assignment was to establish a temporary prisoner of war camp at one end of the Baghdad International Airport. Under Smith's skilled direction, they did just that: punching a hole in a wall with an Armored Combat Earthmover (ACE) and securing the perimeter of a courtyard on the other side. They did their job and they did it well.

Not long after they commandeered the courtyard, they came under fire. Iraqi soldiers, just over one hundred of them, began shooting from a nearby tower and from over the surrounding walls. Many of Sergeant Smith's men were wounded and when he called in a Bradley Fighting Vehicle and an Armored Personnel Carrier, they too took heavy fire and their crews were badly injured.

At this point, the true character of Sergeant Smith shone. He ordered one of his men to back the Armored Personnel Carrier into a strategic position at the end of the courtyard and, while calling for the evacuation of the wounded, he climbed aboard the

SERGEANT PAUL

RAY SMITH

carrier and began returning fire with its 50. caliber machine gun. Almost single-handedly he kept the Iraqis at bay while the wounded were tended and his remaining men found cover. Reports of the incident later concluded that Sergeant Smith killed more than fifty Iraqi soldiers, kept dozens of his men from harm, and inspired those under his command to drive off the enemy.

Sadly, the report also concluded that as Sergeant Smith valiantly protected his men, he took the bullet to the head that ended his life. For his sacrifice, this heroic man would not only receive the undying devotion of his men but would also become the first soldier in the Iraqi conflict to receive the Congressional Medal of Honor. Indeed, when President Bush awarded the medal to Sergeant Smith's widow and children, he concluded by saying, "And we express our gratitude for a new generation of Americans, every bit as selfless and dedicated to liberty as any that has gone on before—a dedication exemplified by the sacrifice and valor of

Sergeant First Class Paul Ray Smith." Truly, Sergeant Smith had lived up to the legacy of the Third Infantry—to the heritage of the "Rock of the Marne," and to the glory of the American soldier he aspired to be.

"WARS MAY BE FOUGHT WITH WEAPONS, BUT THEY ARE WON BY MEN. IT IS THE SPIRIT OF THE MEN WHO FOLLOW AND OF THE MAN WHO LEADS THAT GAINS THE VICTORY."

GENERAL GEORGE S. PATTON

LIVING THE SOLDIER'S CREED

There is an oath that all American soldiers take. It is part of a set of commitments called "The Soldier's Creed." At the heart of this creed is a determination that every soldier contemplates in his quiet hours: "I will never leave a fallen comrade."

Few soldiers, though, have the opportunity to test this determination as Sergeant First Class Gary Villalobos did on June 7, 2005. On that day, Sergeant Villalobos was on patrol in Tal Afar, just ninety miles from the Syrian border. He was serving with a unit assigned to provide support and training for a new Iraqi army brigade. This assignment is what landed him on the streets of Tal Afar with seventeen Iraqi soldiers and Lieutenant Colonel Terrence Crowe.

The squad had just begun their patrol that day when they came under heavy rocket and machine gun fire. One of their number was killed instantly. Searching for a better position, Crowe and Villalobos led the squad down an alley, but they were immediately ambushed by five insurgents. It was terrifying. Bullets rained down on them in torrents. Sergeant Villalobos had never experienced such intense fighting.

In fact, the fighting was so intense that when he looked back at his men he discovered that all but two of the seventeen Iraqi soldiers had fled. The situation was desperate, and then it grew worse. Within moments, Lieutenant Colonel Crowe took several bullets to the stomach.

Instantly, Sergeant Villalobos had a decision to make. There, some ten feet in front of him, lay his dying commander. Above were insurgents unleashing ferocious rocket, grenade, and small arms fire. He had two options. The first, to withdraw, saving his life and the lives of his two men. The second, to risk almost certain death to reclaim Lieutenant Colonel Crowe's body. What should he do?

At that moment the words came back to him: "I will never leave a fallen comrade." Determined now to rescue Crowe, Sergeant Villalobos called for support and proceeded to lead a heated assault on the insurgents. He killed one insurgent with rifle fire and moments later killed the rest by throwing a heavy fragmentation grenade into the enemy's position. He then retrieved his commander's body and rushed him back to a waiting vehicle.

Sergeant Villalobos soon learned that, despite his heroic efforts, Lieutenant Colonel Crowe died of his wounds. He was grieved at the loss of this beloved leader but he was also thankful he had fulfilled his oath to never leave a fallen comrade behind. For his valor, Sergeant Villalobos was awarded the Silver Star, but his greatest reward was in knowing that he had kept his word—he had lived THE SOLDIER'S CREED.

The Soldier's

- I am an American soldier.
- I am a Warrior and a member of a team.
- I serve the people of the United States and live the Army Values.
- I will always place the mission first.
- I will never accept defeat.
- I will never quit.
- I will never leave a fallen comrade.
- I am disciplined, physically and mentally tough, trained and proficient in my warrior tasks and drills.

Creed

- I always maintain my arms, my equipment, and myself.
- I am an expert and I am a professional.
- I stand ready to deploy, engage, and destroy the enemies of the United States of America in close combat.
- I am a guardian of freedom and the American way of life.
- I am an American soldier.

A SOLDIER FINDS HIS COUNTRY

Lieutenant Daniel Morales arrived in Afghanistan with his mind full of the anti-American rage of his university professors. "We are the oppressors," his teachers had insisted. "We are doing only harm to the people of Afghanistan and Iraq." Lieutenant Morales had come to do his duty, then, but could not give his heart to his nation's cause.

That was about to change. On his first day in Afghanistan, he met a medic who had been shot in a skirmish and had then crawled through a hailstorm of bullets to tend the wounds of the very man who shot him.

A week later, Lieutenant Morales watched as an American helicopter flew over a field where Afghan boys were playing. As they had been taught to do, the boys picked up rocks to throw at the Americans. But as they were about to let loose, a soccer ball sailed out

41

of the cargo door of the hovering chopper. Immediately, the boys dropped the rocks and chased after the ball. Soon a raucous soccer game began, but not before the boys happily waved their thanks to the chopper pilots, their angry scowls giving way to joyous smiles.

Several weeks later, Lieutenant Morales happened to be near an engineering unit as they loaded their trucks. When Morales asked what they were about to do, one of the engineers explained that they were about to rebuild a school that insurgents had destroyed days before. "How many times has the school been destroyed?" Morales asked. "Eleven times," was the answer.

"Well, how many times do you intend to rebuild it?" the astonished lieutenant asked. "Till Jesus comes or Osama goes!" said the engineer, his entire crew bursting into laugher. The phrase had apparently become their witty slogan, but they fully intended to live it out.

Finally, when Morales was assigned to his quarters, he noticed that one of his roommates came in from his shift each day completely exhausted. Yet within

MORALES

minutes the man would leave again dressed in an athletic warm-up suit. When Morales questioned his roommate, the tall, quiet black man explained that he was coaching a basketball team of Afghan boys and then teaching them English after their practices. The boys had come to count on him and, as exhausted as he was, he could not let them down.

Lieutenant Morales thought about what he had seen and heard in his few short months in Iraq. Finally, he decided to write one of his professors at home. He told this fiery critic of American foreign policy that what he had seen in Afghanistan did not square with what he had been taught in the professor's class. He said that it was time for both of them, the soldier and the professor, to be true to their principles. Lieutenant Morales said that he was going to remain an American soldier, that he had found it a noble calling. Yet because the professor did not believe in the American cause, Morales suggested he might find another country in which to live. The letter then closed with this line: "I am fighting to liberate a country that seems perfectly suited to your views. I'll tell them to expect you." With these words, Lieutenant Daniel Morales returned to the life he had chosen: the work of an American hero.

COMING HOME AGAIN

When Specialist Justin Johnson was called up to fight in Iraq, his father, Joe, knew what he had to do.

He couldn't let his son go to Iraq alone. After all, Joe had years of experience in the Georgia National Guard.

44

He would ship out too and keep an eye
on him. He had promised his wife
that he would. Then came the bad
news. Joe learned that the
Georgia National Guard wasn't
being called up. Joe was frantic. He
began searching for a guard unit that
was heading for Iraq and finally
found one in Washington State. It was
far away, but at least Joe had found a
way to be near his son overseas.

So while Justin mobilized to
Iraq, Joe traveled to Fort Lewis in
Washington. Then he met another
disappointment. During training, Joe
horribly damaged his knee. The doctors

told him it would require surgery. This meant more delays and more distance between Joe and his son. So he waited and fought mounting frustration.

Then the worst news of all reached Joe in a tearful phone call from his grieving wife. Justin had been on patrol only twelve days after beginning duty in Iraq when his Humvee hit an IED (Improvised Explosive Device). The driver survived, but Justin was killed instantly. The news hit Joe much as the IED hit Justin's Humvee. He was shattered inside, devastated by the loss of his son and by his own sense of failure. He had not been there for Justin.

With Justin dead, should Joe still go to Iraq? He decided that he should. He endured the surgery on his knee, regained his strength, and within a few months shipped out to Iraq with the Washington National Guard.

But something had

changed in Joe. He felt angry and knew he was distant from God. Joe and his wife had been missionaries in South America and they knew what it was to feel the pleasure of God as they served in a foreign land. But now, in Iraq, Joe wasn't sure that he felt anything anymore. He just did his duty and tried to honor the memory of his son.

Yet as much as he had been tempted to surrender to bitterness, Joe found himself coming alive again when he encountered the children of Iraq. Their open hearts and loving eyes drew him back to faith and compassion. With his fellow soldiers, he handed out candy and distributed much-needed school supplies. There was a laugh or two along the way and sometimes he managed to spend a few minutes kicking the soccer ball around. Joe Johnson found his heart again.

Joe still wears a bracelet that reminds him of his son's violent death in Iraq. It reads: "April 10, 2004. Spc. Justin Johnson, 22." Now, though, he is not serving a vengeful purpose overseas. Instead, he honors his son as his Christian faith tells him he should: by loving, by defending, and by serving. It isn't hard for him now. He has reclaimed his more noble self by loving the children of Iraq.

The
SOLDIER'S
Psalm

BLESSED BE THE LORD MY ROCK,

WHO TRAINS MY HANDS FOR WAR,

AND MY FINGERS FOR BATTLE—

MY LOVINGKINDNESS AND MY FORTRESS,

MY HIGH TOWER AND MY DELIVERER,

MY SHIELD AND THE ONE IN WHOM I TAKE REFUGE,

WHO SUBDUES MY PEOPLE UNDER ME.

Psalm 144:1–2

Message from a HERO

On Memorial Day, May 30, 2005, Corporal Jeffrey Starr took a sniper's bullet in the chest during a skirmish in Ar Ramadi, Iraq. The bullet came to rest in his heart and ended his life. His flag-draped coffin was returned to his parents in Snohomish, Washington.

Two months later, a letter from Jeffrey reached his family. He had written it on his laptop computer and saved it in a file entitled "LetterHome." The computer that contained the letter had been stored at Camp Pendleton, California, along with Jeffrey's other belongings. The young marine knew that if he died his parents and his girlfriend would eventually retrieve his computer, read his letter, and know his heart.

His words would express not only what was in his heart, but in the hearts of thousands like him.

I'm writing this for one reason only. On April 13th, 2004, I thought I was going to die. My only regret is that I hadn't spent enough time with you. That I hadn't told you everything I wanted to. Being in Iraq for a 3rd time, I don't want to feel that way again because it was the worst feeling ever.

So this letter is in case I won't ever get the chance to tell you "I don't regret going, everybody dies but few get to do it for something as important as freedom. It may seem confusing why we are in Iraq, it's not to me. I'm here helping these people so that they can live the way we live. Not have to worry about tyrants or vicious dictators. To do what they want with their lives. To me that is why I died. Others have died for my freedom, now this is my mark."

I love you with all of my heart.
Goodbye...

With these words, Corporal Jeffrey Starr not only bid farewell to his girlfriend and his family, but he also defined the meaning of the war for many in his generation. He gave voice to the attitude of sacrifice that has defined the best of America's heroes since our nation began.

DIGGING A WELL OF INSPIRATION

MSGT Russ Laporte

I can do all things through Christ who strengthens me.
Phil. 4:13

Kenny Vaughan is not a soldier. He is a long-distance water-ski jumper. He is not stationed in Afghanistan or Iraq. He lives in Beaumont, Texas. Yet his battle to conquer an enemy of his soul has meant inspiration for thousands on America's battlefields, and so it is that his story is linked now with the story of the American hero.

Kenny had the potential to be among the top long-distance water-ski jumpers in the country. He was good, very good, and he wanted to be the best.

So, like all athletes who dream of championships, Kenny worked hard, refusing to be satisfied with his last performance.

He knew his conditioning and his skills were ready for the ultimate challenge, but something was working against his soul that threatened to bring defeat. It was fear. Though he had known many successes, fear of failure crippled Kenny. He heard its haunting voice as he suited up for a competition or as he sped toward the ramp before a jump. It distracted him, taunted him, and drained him of the courage and concentration he needed to do his best.

Kenny had almost decided he would never conquer this

fear when he read Matthew 21:22: "Whatever things you ask in prayer, believing, you will receive."

Kenny realized that if he truly trusted his God, he should ask for freedom from the fear that was robbing him and then trust that the answer would come. Kenny understood that his job was simply to have faith. And it worked. The fear that had robbed him of so much in his life began leaving his soul.

Some months later, Kenny went to the USA Water-Ski National Championships. Though he tore a ski boot in his second attempt, his third attempt was good enough to win the championship. Kenny Vaughan fulfilled his dream of being one of the best long-distance water-ski jumpers in the nation.

Asked about it afterward, Kenny said that one of the reasons he jumped so far was that on the third attempt, when fear might have gripped him, he looked down and saw that his wife had written a scripture on his tow rope. It made all the difference, and he rode that wave of faith to victory.

Kenny had learned the power of words, particularly the words of the Bible, to inspire the human heart in the heat of battle. In time he decided to put words of inspiration on dog tags so others who strove to be champions could wear them and be strengthened in their faith. Kenny's brother thought of a name for the little dog tags: Shields of Strength, based on the Bible verse that describes God as a shield and a strength to the faithful, Psalm 28:7.

Kenny could not have been prepared for what happened next. The Shields of Strength became wildly popular. He could hardly keep up with the demand.

Greater love hath no man than this, that a man lay down his life for his friends.
John 15:13

I will be strong and courageous. I will not be terrified, or discouraged; for the Lord my God is with me wherever I go.
Joshua 1:9

Shields of Strength

AFC

United States of America
One Nation Under God

What moved him most, though, was the demand for the Shields of Strength among soldiers overseas. Tens of thousands of the little dog tags are now in Afghanistan and Iraq. Soldiers carry them in their pockets or around their necks. They recite the verses on them and even kiss them before battle as a touchstone of faith.

They are more than trinkets of belief, though. Captain Russell Rippetoe, whose story is told in this book, was carrying a Shield of Strength in his pocket when he was killed in Iraq. When the Smithsonian Museum put Rippetoe's gear on display, the Shield of Strength—burned

at the edges from the explosion that killed the captain—was a testimony to the young officer's faith.

Likewise, Lieutenant Daniel Morales carried a Shield of Strength. When he wrote his university professor and challenged him to rethink the meaning of America's cause in the war, he put a Shield of Strength in the envelope. It was one of the best ways he knew to show the professor what he believed.

There are *thousands* of soldiers like Rippetoe and Morales who draw inspiration for combat from a little piece of metal that reminds them of their faith and a God who is near. And it all began when Kenny Vaughan decided not to let fear control his life. Now, he has dug a well of faith and inspiration for American soldiers around the world.

"*Their story is known to all of you. It is the story of the American man at arms. My estimate of him was formed on the battlefields many, many years ago, and has never changed. I regarded him then, as I regard him now, as one of the world's noblest figures.*"

GENERAL DOUGLAS MACARTHUR

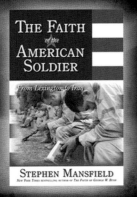

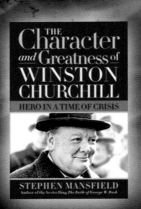
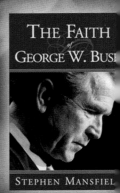

Shields of Strength®

I will be strong and courageous. I will not be terrified, or discouraged; for the Lord my God is with me wherever I go.
Joshua 1:9

...yer of Salvation
Dear Lord Jesus,
I realize I am a sinner,
I repent for my sins,
and right this moment
I receive You as my
Lord and Savior. Amen

Shields of Strength

If you would like to review other designs and receive a free Shields of Strength catalog, please call **1.800.326.7882** or visit **www.shieldsofstrength.com**.

ere is one in the Oval Office, others in the pockets of congressmen and senators, and, aside from the official ignias they wear, it is the emblem most often carried by members of the military in Afghanistan and Iraq."

— Stephen Mansfield, Author: *The Faith of the American Soldier & The Faith of George W. Bush*